Fire Truck Factory

Catherine Anderson

Heinemann Library
Chicago, Illinois

Customer Service 888-454-2279
Visit our website at www.heinemannlibrary.com

Page Layout by Kim Kovalick, Heinemann Library
Printed and bound in China by South China Printing Company Limited.
Photo research by Jill Birschbach

09 08 07 06 05
10 9 8 7 6 5 4 3 2 1

Library of Congress Cataloging-in-Publication Data
Anderson, Catherine, 1974-
  Fire truck factory / Catherine Anderson.
      p. cm. -- (Field trip!)
  Includes index.
  ISBN 1-4034-6162-7 (HC), 1-4034-6168-6 (Pbk.)
  1. Fire engines--Juvenile literature. 2. Factories--Juvenile literature. [1. Fire engines. 2. Factories.] I. Title. II. Series.
  TH9372.A52 2004
  629.225--dc22

                                  2003027859

Acknowledgments
The author and publishers are grateful to the following for permission to reproduce copyright material:
p. 4 George Hall/Corbis; pp. 5, 6, 7, 8, 9, 10, 11, 12, 13, 14, 15, 16, 17, 18, 20, 23, back cover Robert Lifson/Heinemann Library; p. 19 George Hall/Corbis; p. 21 Photodisc Green/Getty Images

Cover photograph by Robert Lifson/Heinemann Library

Every effort has been made to contact copyright holders of any material reproduced in this book. Any omissions will be rectified in subsequent printings if notice is given to the publisher.

Special thanks to George Kanugh and Seagrave Fire Apparatus in Clintonville, Wisconsin, for their help in the preparation of this book.

Special thanks to our advisory panel for their help in the preparation of this series:

Alice Bethke
Library Consultant
Palo Alto, California

Malena Bisanti-Wall
Media Specialist
American Heritage Academy
Canton, Georgia

Ellen Dolmetsch, MLS
Tower Hill School
Wilmington, Delaware

Contents

Some words are shown in bold, **like this.**
You can find them in the picture glossary on page 23.

Where Do Fire Trucks Come From?

You may have seen a fire truck racing down the street.

They are special trucks that help put out fires.

Fire trucks are made in factories.

Workers put together all the different parts.

What Are the Different Parts of a Fire Truck?

cab pump module

The cab is where the firefighters sit to drive the truck.

The **pump** module is where the firefighters control the pump.

ladder

body

The body holds the water tank.

Some fire trucks have an aerial device, such as a ladder.

How Do They Make the Cab?

Workers **weld** the pieces of the cab together.

The cab looks like a big box.

door

The workers put the doors on the cab, too.

The cab has to be strong to protect the firefighters.

How Do They Make the Body?

Workers **weld** the pieces of the body together.

The body looks like a long rectangle.

Then, the cab and the body
are painted.

They are usually painted red.

How Do the Parts Go Together?

frame rail

The workers can start to put the truck together.

The frame rail will hold up all the parts of the truck.

axle

The axles fit on the frame rail.

The tires fit on the axles.

What Does the Engine Look Like?

The frame rail holds the **engine,** too.

A big fire truck needs a big engine!

The cab covers the engine.

The frame rail holds the **pump** module, too.

What Does the Pump Module Do?

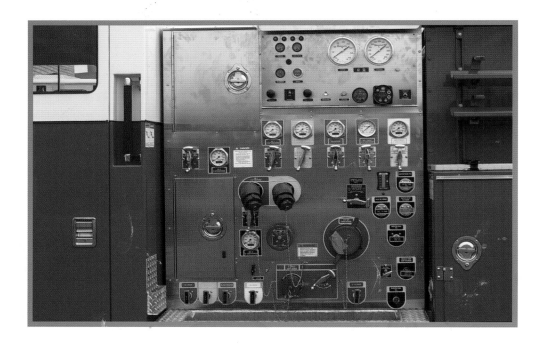

The **pump** module has controls.

The controls work the pump.

A firefighter uses the pump to
spray water on a fire.

What Is an Aerial Device?

An aerial device can be a ladder.

Ladders are made at the factory, too.

The ladders go on top of
the trucks.

They help the firefighters reach
high places.

What Happens to the Fire Trucks Next?

Workers at the factory make sure the finished trucks work well.

They check all the different parts of the trucks.

The trucks go to fire departments all over the country.

Then, firefighters get to use their new trucks!

Fire Truck Map

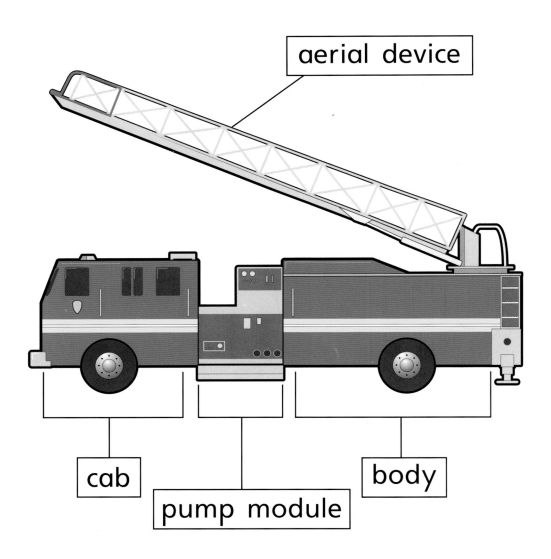

aerial device

cab

pump module

body

Picture Glossary

engine
pages 14, 15
machine that makes something move

pump
pages 6, 16, 17
thing that pushes liquids, like water, from one place to another

weld
pages 8, 10
to connect two metals together

Note to Parents and Teachers

Reading for information is an important part of a child's literacy development. Learning begins with a question about something. Help children think of themselves as investigators and researchers by encouraging their questions about the world around them. Each chapter in this book begins with a question. Read the question together. Look at the pictures. Talk about what you think the answer might be. Then read the text to find out if your predictions were correct. Think of other questions you could ask about the topic, and discuss where you might find the answers. Assist children in using the picture glossary and the index to practice new vocabulary and research skills.

Index